UNITY

THE EVOLUTION OF CONSCIOUSNESS

UNITY

THE EVOLUTION OF CONSCIOUSNESS

This book is dedicated
To the light within all
Know the truth
In unity we stand tall

TABLE OF CONTENTS

PART 1: HEARTBEAT OF THE EARTHMOTHER

Nature: A Prayer For Peace   11
Sol   15
Home Is Where The Heart Is   19
Wildflower   23
Polyamorphous Rhythms   27
Mother Nature   31
The Flow Of Life   35
Heartbeat Of The Earthmother   39
Treedom   43
Luna   47
Mama Bear   51
Essence Of The Mountain   55

PART 2: DARK KNIGHT OF THE SOUL

Heart: A Prayer For Love   63
The Way I See It   67
What It Means To Be Human   71
Broken   75
No One Else Like You   79
Kindred Spirits   83
The Darkness   87
With Love   91
A New Day   93
Working Man   97
Wanderer   101
The Flame   105

PART 3: LIGHTBEARER

Light: A Prayer For Unity	111
Inward Movement	115
Starseed	119
The Nomad	123
The Path	125
The Wizard	129
One Love	133
Breathe	137
Lionheart	141
Earth Angel	145
Today Is The Day	149
Being Of Light	153

PART 1:

HEARTBEAT OF THE EARTHMOTHER

NATURE: A PRAYER FOR PEACE

By observing Mother Nature we can learn to attain greater peace. Peace is the natural state of all that exists. In nature nothing is ever rushed as everything unfolds when it is ready. Therein lies peace. All cycles come to completion when the time is right. The past and future see destruction and creation, the present sees eternity.

Inner peace comes through self understanding. When you take the time and focused attention to understand yourself you are able to love yourself more fully. By residing in the present moment you allow peace to be brought forth from within. Simply allow yourself to be.

When we live in accordance with nature we experience harmony. It is up to each of us to look within ourselves so that we can discover our true nature. You are an expresssion of a bountiful creative energy that has no boundaries. The same cosmic forces that shape our Earth also end up shaping you.

Nature creates without limits
So what's stopping you
From showing the world your inner beauty
And all that you can do

Self realization is the natural movement of all beings. Just as all rivers flow to the ocean, all life moves towards the divine. Even though your journey may seem different, know that all destinations are the same. Just like the trees, we are all reaching for the light. It is through this that we come to know ourselves.

Nature reminds us that we are all part of a larger whole. We are all connected in the web of life. Step foward with courage and grace and know that you are part of the infinite whole. Know that you can feel the completion you've been searching for your entire life.

Contemplate the beauty in a single grain of sand and in the magnificence of a mountain. Come to appreciate the large and small acts of love in your life. Allow your actions to be in service and step forward on the path of unity. Allow yourself to feel deeply connected to your essence and all of life and you will discover the truth.

Nature is a great teacher
Don't forget what it has shown
Open your heart to the world
And you will never be alone

13

SOL

As the sun rises
And day begins to break
The Earth becomes alive
And creatures begin to wake

Reflections of light
Pass before my face
The wind wraps the Earth
In a loving embrace

As a breeze laps the curtails
Of a lone butterfly
Floating effortlessly
Into the sky

I realize how complex
Life can be
Infinite systems
Comprise reality

Yet how can it be
That all of this is here
We have been given so much
But it still isn't clear

How all of this
Can exist as one
Perfect harmony
Under the sun

HOME IS WHERE THE HEART IS

Let your arms reach out to embrace the world
The way the branches of a tree touch the sky
For life is short
And all too soon you will die

Let your spirit nourish the world
The way water nourishes the earth
It will teach you how to give without expectation
Show you what life is really worth

Learn to let go
Be as easy as the breeze
And you will come to find
That you can do anything you please

Let your life flow
Like a winding stream
Your future is unknown
Don't be afraid to dream

Follow your breath
As it goes in, and as it comes out
Like the tides of an ocean
Dissolving all doubt

Use your enthusiasm
To help others shine bright
The way a roaring fire
Illuminates the night

Don't be afraid
To take a chance
The way the leaves in autumn
Weave and dance

Nature is a great teacher
Don't forget what it has shown
Open your heart to the world
And you will never be alone

WILDFLOWER

From the earth
A seedling breaks
Roots take hold
As she awakes

She asks for nothing
As she creeps into the sky
Content with the glowing sun
As the days go by

Battered hard
By the wind and the rain
She sits on a mountain top
And feels no pain

For she has seen
Much sorrow in life
Found joy inside
And ended her strife

Not every flower
Is ever so bold
To find in herself
A heart of gold

WILDFLOWER

As she starts to radiate
Eternal love
Petals shoot from her
Like the stars above

She shines brightly
For all to see
Her immense beauty
Alive and free

For she started
As we all do
A little seedling
Who grew and grew

Open to the world
Like the valleys below
Infinite possibilities
To learn and grow

Creating beauty
In a gentle spring shower
Who thought so much could come
From such a little flower

POLYAMORPHOUS RHYTHMS

Blood pumps
Heart beats
Rolling along
Like fields of wheat

Sun rises
Light shines
Day after day
Ticking time

Waves curl
Crash and break
Stripping shoreline
Give and take

Moon glows
Darkness creeps
Blanketing Earth
Animals sleep

Leaves whisper
Touched by wind
Carrying secrets
Let them in

Fire leaps
It knows no bounds
Cleanse your soul
Move to higher ground

Earth spins
Like a top
Round and round
It never stops

Feel the rhythm
Before its too late
Death plays its part
In sealing your fate

MOTHER NATURE

Oh, my sweet dear
Why must you go
You know it breaks my heart
To see you so

When I first met you
It was love at first sight
You captured my soul
And stole off into the night

Your radiant beauty
Leaves me in awe
Completely dumbfounded
At what I just saw

I yearn to hear your voice again
As gentle as a summer breeze
One murmur from you
Would drop me to my knees

To touch your endearing lips
A euphoric kiss
Ensuring Cupid's arrow
Will not miss

A wild seductress
I am putty in your hands
As you capture the hearts of men at home
And those in faraway lands

Oh Mother Nature
Why must you go
You know it breaks my heart
To see you so

THE FLOW OF LIFE

Life is like a river
Always flowing
Always changing

Finding it's true nature
In temporal experience
From one moment
To the next

Eventually
There will be a moment
When the river
Meets the ocean
Returning itself
To the Source

As one river ends
Another begins
As clouds shed anew
Allowing life
To continue

THE FLOW OF LIFE

Experiencing everything
As it is
Always flowing
Always changing
From one moment
To the next

HEARTBEAT OF THE EARTHMOTHER

Turn off the voice
Of those around you
And turn off
Your own voice

Only then will you hear
The Universal Voice

It's in the trees
And the breeze
And the birds
Around you

It is a voice that you will only hear
In silence

And it is waiting to speak with you
It wants to share it's secrets
But you must be willing to listen

Many will pass this by
But you will stop and wonder
You can hear her softly now
Calling your name

And as you draw nearer
And let her wild spirit take over
You can hear her closer
Whispering in your ear

The Earthmother comes
with such grace, such fragility
That you are captivated
By her very presence

Her essence runs through you
And you become whole again
Everything around you changes
As you see it for the first time

She will open your heart
And she will open your mind
And show you
Just how much a part of life
You really are

When she tells you her secrets
You will feel it

In every pore of your body
And every bone
Immersed with her
And with all life

You will see her
In each cosmic wave of grass
And feel her hold you
The way a root clings to the earth

When you are together
Life is beautiful

And when you are apart
You feel her presence close to you
Beating in your heart

TREEDOM

Be like a tree
And stand firmly
Ground yourself
In the experience of life

As you extend your branches
Into the sky
And your roots
Into the ground

Know that you
Are the primordial link
Between Heaven
And Earth

Energy flows through you
From the wind
And the sun
And the rain

Stand tall and be proud
Like a Douglas Fir
Nature created you perfectly
Because she know's no other way

Be open
To any possibility
The way the buds of a fresh sapling
Open to the sun's rays

Keep your skin hard
Like the bark of an Oak
For you will be weathered
By life's trials

Seasons will pass
You will begin to wither
Your body may collapse
But your soul will linger

To help revitalize
All things on this Earth
Sometimes one life must end
To give another birth

LUNA

Luna, Goddess
Show me the path
For thou art with me
My rod and my staff

Illuminate the darkness
For all to see
The beauty of nature
Our divinity

Rising above
When we cast stones
Lifting us up
When we are alone

Holding the Earth
In a loving embrace
Drinking the tide
Slipping through space

As you emerge
From your long dark curtain
Helping me now
I know I am certain

To find what I have been searching for
All this time
Understanding, meaning
Can it be mine?

To show others
These teachings of yours
To climb the mountain
To unlock the door

Love permeates
All of God's creatures
Illuminating ourselves
And all the Earth's features

Enlighten our world
Make it your home
Leaving dogma
Sitting alone

Follow me now
Enter the temple
Bridging through space
Our body the vessel

MAMA BEAR

There's a woman I know
They call her Mama Bear
Protector and guardian
With the world in her care

Never before
Have I met such a giver
Her heart overflows
Like a raging river

Spreading love and peace
Everywhere she goes
Into the deepest cracks
Of the iciest flows

A divine being
A warrior goddess of light
Her eyes glow like the moon
On a starlit night

Hiding mysteries and stories
Better left untold
She radiates like the sun
With a heart of gold

MAMA BEAR

Standing tall and proud
Like a mighty cedar
Rooted in love
She's a fearless leader

Always willing to help
Show others the way
Solid like a mountain
She does not stray

Her spirit calms and nourishes
Purified by the fire
Capturing the hearts of many
As the flames burn higher

A healer and a lover
A mother of the earth
Exploring the depths of Spirit
To find what life is really worth

Radiating calm and peace
Like the waves of an ocean
Her vibration speaks
To her well of devotion

An angel and a seer
A mother and a guide
She embraces this world
With her heart open wide

She's wild and free
Like the wind in her hair
And that's why they call her
Mama Bear

ESSENCE OF THE MOUNTAIN

As the sun rises
Above towering peaks
Foot to the earth
To find what you seek

Freedom and peace
From the day to day
Walk the path
And find the way

As you rise above
Who you used to be
The air gets thinner
It's easier to see

How far you've come
To be where you are
A perfect unfolding
Like a shooting star

Life is designed
Completely by you
Follow your heart
And find what is true

Driven by desire
An indomitable will
Life doesn't always have to be
A slog uphill

Sometimes you'll get
A breeze in the trees
Let go of attachment
And find the ease

It's so much easier
When there's less to carry
Just know that letting go
Is kinda scary

Bring some friends
Who will lend their ears
And have the courage
To face your fears

As you peer from the top
So infinite and vast
You create your future
By leaving the past

It won't take
As long as you think
As night sets in
The stars start to wink

An infinite galaxy
Lies above
Bringing to light
The path of love

PART 2:

DARK KNIGHT OF THE SOUL

HEART: A PRAYER FOR LOVE

Every soul on this earth yearns for love. It is the spiritual life force that sustains us. We all need it to survive and thrive as individuals, and as a species. The love you have inside of you is the greatest gift you have to offer the world. Now more than ever we need you to share your gifts. People are suffering, the world is suffering and you are here to teach them love.

Listen to your heart and let it be your guiding light. Your feelings are the voice of your inner teacher and your higher self. Allow them to guide you. Trust the intuitive guidance you receive. You are being led down your divine life path. It is only through listening that you will discover that which can lead you toward ultimate truth.

It is up to you to make your own choices and decisions in life. This is your responsibility and your blessing. You always have the power of choice. It is up to you how you use it.

Trust in yourself
And you will go far
More than anyone else
You know who you are

You will face challenges in life. Know that every experience is here for you to learn from. Trust that the same hand that guides the universe is also guiding you. Know that everything will come together in the best possible way, at the best possible time, for your highest soul growth.

In this moment you can choose to see things differently. Choose to see through the eyes of love and find forgiveness for yourself and others. Forgivness is practice in unconditional love.

While you are witnessing the ascent of grace your soul will go through trials and tribulations. These are meant to teach you lessons that will allow you to live more in tune with the rhythms of your heart. The darkness exists so that we can understand the light. Like a phoenix rising from the ashes it will transform you. Surrender all that you think you are and you will discover your immortal nature.

It is only in our darkest moments
That we can truly see
The light that lies inside of us
So we can set it free

THE WAY I SEE IT

You're the girl I'd hoped for
All those years
Cold winter nights
And lonely fears

But your heart warms me
Like the sun warms the earth
Able to show me
What life is really worth

Through your thoughts and your actions
Your hopes and your dreams
You have me moving along
Like a winding stream

Flowing endlessly
A weave through space
Time no longer exists
In this place

When I'm with you
I'm one and I'm whole
Embracing everything
Deep in my soul

A connection to the Earth
Energy aligned
A girl like you
So hard to find

You can teach me more
Than I could learn on my own
Lessons of the divine
From you, I'm shown

Your heart radiates
With eternal love
It shines so pure
Like the glow of a dove

You have the innocence
Of a child
Bringing the world to life
It drives me wild

You create
With the hand of God
Always perfected
And never flawed

Eternally grateful
That I have met you
Always hoped to find
A love that was true

Together now
And it feels so right
With the moon shining above
In the dark of the night

WHAT IT MEANS TO BE HUMAN

Sometimes we forget
What it means to feel
Dead to the world
Like nothing is real

Open yourself up
To the sea of emotion
Feel the pull
Like the tides of the ocean

Sometimes you don't know
Which way you will go
Who you will meet
How you will grow

Life flies by
Way too fast
Live for today
Don't regret the past

We all make
Mistakes in life
Learn to forgive
And end this strife

If I knew
I would die tomorrow
I wouldn't feel pain
Or sadness, or sorrow

I would spend today
With the one I love
Hold her in my arms
Under the sky above

We would laugh and talk
Deep into the night
I would hold her close
With all my might

And feel her touch
Burning my skin
Nuzzling up
Her face to my chin

I would peer deeply
Into her eyes
Kiss her gently
Until the darkness dies

As the silence of the dawn
Creeps through the still air
I'd cradle her softly
Run my hands through her hair

Then we would see
The first rays of light
Feel the warmth on our skin
And smile with delight

Grateful for the time
That we had spent together
As I begin to leave this world
And break this mortal tether

I hope that when I'm gone
She won't be lonely
She needs to know
That she's my one and only

BROKEN

Words cannot describe
How I feel
No matter how much I try
This doesn't seem real

It's so hard to watch
Your love walk away
When you're hoping desperately
That she will stay

I haven't felt an emptiness
Like this before
I never expected
That this was in store

It feels so cold
Like a bleak autumn rain
And I'm not sure
How to deal with the pain

I always thought we would be
Together for life
I dreamed that one day
I'd make you my wife

BROKEN

But now I feel
Gripped in despair
Knowing that tomorrow
You won't be there

I miss you so much
It's hard to sleep
I close my eyes
But they just weep

Broken inside
I feel so blue
Cause I know that deep down
My heart's still with you

NO ONE ELSE LIKE YOU

She cared about me
More than anyone ever has before
It felt so good to be loved
I could never have asked for more

I've never had anything
That has warmed my heart so much
As the beauty of her smile
And the radiance of her touch

Sometimes when I enter my room
And breath that all familiar smell
It makes me dream of her
And my heart starts to swell

I still think about her
Every single day
Even though I know
Life will go it's own way

I'm sorry I didn't love her
The way she wanted to feel
I hope that she forgives me
And we both find a way to heal

NO ONE ELSE LIKE YOU

It's hard to walk out
And embrace the unknown
No one wants
To spend life all alone

I still wish
That she was right there
So I could hold her close
Run my hands through her hair

Tell her how much she means to me
Because I know my love was true
I can spend a lifetime searching
But there is no one else like you

KINDRED SPIRITS

There will be times when life
Will beat you down
Pushed off the deep end
And left to drown

Sinking lower and lower
Gasping for air
Feelings of misery
As you're consumed by despair

You're not sure
If you can go on
Will's put to the test
When all hope is gone

When you're wandering alone
Fumbling in the dark
All it takes is a friend
To ignite the spark

To bring you up
When you feel weak
To appreciate you
And listen when you speak

To give you courage
When you no longer have strength
People who would do anything
And go to any length

Make sure you tell them
How much you care
They'll stand up for you
When life's too much to bear

I just want to thank
All these friends of mine
Your presence is a blessing
Your company, divine

THE DARKNESS

There are moments in life
When you will feel weak
Not sure where to go
Not sure what you seek

Nothing seems to matter
You don't seem to care
Carrying the weight of the world
Is just too much to bear

Even though it seems
That only dark times lay ahead
You must have hope for the future
So you don't get wrapped in dread

It is only in our darkest moments
That we can truly see
The light that lies inside of us
So we can set it free

To break the shackles
Of this mental prison
And allow you to accept
The new you that's arisen

Bolder, better
Stronger than before
Nothing causes you to grow
Like getting stripped down to the core

Have faith in life
Let it guide your way
For all too soon
The night becomes day

And once again
The path becomes clear
You no longer have to live your life
Consumed by fear

WITH LOVE

We both know
We have to go our own way
As the winds of change blow
And we begin a new day

You made me a better person
I know this to be true
I'm ten times the man I used to be
And I owe it all to you

I hope that you will find
Whatever it is you seek
And know that when I think of you
I'll see you only at your peak

Your life will challenge you
Put your resolve to the test
Just know as your journey unfolds
I wish you all the best

A NEW DAY

Waking up
An hour before dawn
Realizing that the one you love
Is really gone

When you are falling from grace
The pace can be violent
So hard to center yourself
Until you are silent

I know how it feels
To be cold and alone
Scared to go out
And live a life on my own

But today is a new day
And I'm living free
Life is so beautiful
And it's easy to see

You need to seize the day
And follow your dreams
Sometimes life really isn't
As hard as it seems

I'm so grateful for everything
That I've been given
The chance to experience
The life I've been living

Instead of letting my heart
Go empty and cold
To live a life of misery
Until I grow old

I want to be the flame
That ignites the spark
For everyone wandering
Alone in the dark

I want to breathe life
Into everyone I meet
Friends and family
And those I see on the street

I want to be the hand
That lifts everyone above
To show them what it means
To truly feel love

Life is an experience
That we all share
Now I'm ready to show the world
How much I care

Because I only have
Love to give
And that will never stop
As long as I live

WORKING MAN

When you start the day
Thinking life is a drag
Dreading work
Your spirits will sag

Is this your choice?
Is this your fate?
What are you to do
In a world consumed by hate

Worrying all day
About what's to come
You never see why
You feel so glum

When you leave the present
To serve loftier notions
Your body is empty
Just going through the motions

Instead of seeing everything
As if it were new
You'll never believe what you've missed
If only you knew...

It shouldn't matter
What you choose to do
Loving everyone
Should be a part of you

No matter your occupation
Your colour, your creed
Love is something
That we all need

So reach out and help
You have nothing to fear
Help those close to you
So they don't shed a tear

We all wonder
What we can change
When we're so confused
That everything seems strange

You don't understand
The power you hold
To turn crumpled hearts
Into polished gold

Sometimes all we need
Is the flash of your smile
Shining like the rays of the sun
In the eyes of a child

To brighten our day
Help our spirits take flight
Let us wash away the gray
And illuminate the night

WANDERER

You hold onto this world
With the arms of a mother
Holding her newborn baby
A love like no other

Clutching desperately
To everything you hold dear
As time passes
Year after year

Things change so fast
In the blink of an eye
Scared to stop and smell the roses
Before life passes you by

We're all on this rock together
We don't know what to do
Our existence is transient
We're all just passing through

Like grains of sand
Spread along the shore
Life is a chance
You couldn't ask for more

WANDERER

You are unique
In every way
One in a billion
Or so they say

You get to experience
What it means to be alive
Why settle for anything less
When you can reach and strive

Nobody knows
What they are capable of
Until they are forced to change
And push comes to shove

Life seems so simple
When we are faced with death
Grounded to the world
Rooted in our breath

Coming to greet us
Then fading away
Reminding us again
Nothing is here to stay

Making us consider
Our own mortality
Teaching us how to live
In this reality

Follow your heart
Learn and grow
For a day will come
When you will let it all go

THE FLAME

The spark is lit
A flash of light
Spark turns to flame
In the night

The flame burns
Creating like the Sun
All things on this Earth
Existing as one

The flame burns
Higher and higher
Reaching and striving
Alive with desire

The flame roars
A furious peak
Living life to the fullest
Is not for the meek

The flame begins to wear
Burning slow
The memories begin to fade
The people come and go

THE FLAME

Burning lower and lower
Gasping for air
Dying slowly
Does anyone care?

The flame dies out
The spark fades away
A transient experience
Nothing is here to stay

The cycle of life continues
Mother Nature moves on
Birds will continue to sing
Long after you're gone

So live in the moment
In this you trust
Ashes to ashes
And dust to dust

PART 3:

LIGHTBEARER

LIGHT: A PRAYER FOR UNITY

Unity is born of peace and love. This is the ultimate teaching of all major world religions and spiritual paths. It is the underlying principle behind all life.

There are many in this world who feel emptiness, a lack of meaning. At this moment in time much of humanity is stuck in the energy of the first three chakras and they are focused on survival, desire, and power. It is now time that we rise to the heart chakra and realize the bountiful gifts we have to offer this world. Give wholeheartedly and you will receive the infinite abundance of the universe.

Life is a journey and love is the destination. It is the destination for us all. As you work towards shining the light of consciousness on the world you will show others the way simply through your way of being. Your presence is a gift and this alone has the ability to illuminate others to new levels of understanding and awareness.

Never underestimate your power
To change someone's day
Teach them love
And show them the way

One who understands the way knows that life is an act of service towards the highest good of all. Have the courage to be a torchbearer and allow your love and light to illuminate all in your life and beyond. Let your presence be a blessing to others and in turn you will be blessed.

Allow your creativity to flow and express the beauty within you. Creation is an act of divine will. It is up to you to share your unique talents and abilities.

You are a bearer of light and now it is time for us to rise in unity. Allow the lotus of your heart centre to blossom as it is illuminated in the divine nature of your soul. Unity is a call to rise together into a new way of being. Where all actions are born from love, peace, and understanding. We are being called to change and it is up to each of us to find the courage within to do what we know we must. Unity consciousness will see love rising to the forefront of human thought.

You were given this light
So that you could shine
Awaken the others
And serve the divine

INWARD MOVEMENT

As you move through this world
Take it in slow
Look inside yourself
It is all you will ever know

Listen to the silence
As it seeps from every pore of the land
The more you pay attention
The more you will understand

Nature creates without limits
So what's stopping you
From showing the world your inner beauty
And all that you can do

You do not know
The power you hold
It goes against everything
You have been told

Everyone is so quick to tell you
How you will fail
But fortune rewards those brave enough
To step beyond the veil

The land beyond
Is found deep within
It is only there you will find peace
And rise above the din

When you find love in this world
And make that special connection
Know that all you see
Is merely your own reflection

Step outside yourself
And take a look inside
Go deep where your spirit waits
And let it be your guide

STARSEED

JUSTIN WESENBERG

From wandering stardust
Life appears
Evolving slowly
For billions of years

Changing it's face
As the cosmos dance
That we would be here
What is the chance

Nobody else will experience
The joy of being you
So appreciate yourself
It's the least you can do

For all too soon
Your body will fade
A soul laid to rest
A journey made

Like a seedling
You will learn and grow
Will you be satisfied
When it's time to let go

If life ever feels
Like it's a grind
Remember your experience
Is one of a kind

So embrace life
The beauty of all things
Give freely to others
Feel the wholeness it brings

As the dusk fades
And your body turns to dust
A supernova ripples out
Another star combusts

THE NOMAD

The Nomad travels lightly
Taking only what he needs
Living free from burden
He moves about with ease

Traveling far and wide
To hidden lands, untold
Wandering out to the sea
And through fields of gold

Abundance follows the Nomad
As he walks his path alone
Content with all he receives
As he makes the Earth his home

His spirit of adventure
Burns deep like a fire
Opening himself up to the world
He fulfills his desire

To experience the world
From a different perspective
To follow his own path
Not the social collective

THE PATH

When you are faced
With the paradox of choice
It can be hard to find what you want
When you can't find your voice

Paths are sprawled out in front of you
Leading every which way
Will you choose your own
Or be led astray

By the whims and callings
That others will make
Sometimes they will pull too much
And cause you to break

Trust in yourself
And you will go far
More than anyone else
You know who you are

Don't become a breeding ground
For doubt and self hate
Let go of this absurdity
And drop this dead weight

THE PATH

Nothing is lacking
Inside of you
I wish you could see yourself
The way that I do

Be who you were born to be
Don't be afraid
Embarrassed or ashamed
At the choices you've made

When you leave this world
And the curtains are drawn
How do you want to be remembered
When you are long gone

Your life is your story
Each day is a page
You only have this moment
To act it on stage

So stop living
In fear and self doubt
Celebrate the journey
It's what life's all about

THE WIZARD

The Wizard sits
As the forest sings
Stars shine brightly
Unknown what the night brings

A master of magic
Tempest of the arcane
Seeking the wisdom of old
Knowledge to gain

He flips patiently
Through an ancient tome
Contemplating diligently
Sitting alone

The Ancients had discovered
The path to follow
Guiding men to divinity
From a life that was hollow

But the teachings were hidden
And hard to find
Locked away
From prying minds

THE WIZARD

Only those who are able
To crack the code
Will find the knowledge they seek
From the masters of old

And there is only one secret
To solving the mystery
But don't look back
It doesn't reside in history

All the knowledge you seek
You will find inside
It's been there all along
With nothing to hide

ONE LOVE

Concept of self
Washes away
Like the pull of the tide
Lapping the bay

Mind is clear
Now that self is gone
Harmoniously empty
Until the coming dawn

With this clearness
Mind can see
All that exists
In your reality

Nothing in this world
Is seperate from you
So hard to change
Your point of view

After being told
Your entire life
What you should think
And what view was right

And once you feel
One and fulfilled
You can stop stagnating
And begin to build

A better life
For all things on this Earth
They're with you now
They've been with you since birth

Nurturing you
Letting you grow
Planting the seeds
For you to sow

As you continue
Putting wheels in motion
A constant rhythm
Like the dance of the ocean

Don't forget
Why you are here
To help out everything
That you hold dear

Don't lose sight
Of what you love
Or it will fly away
Like a passing dove

And leave you
Empty and cold
A desolate void
As you grow old

Enjoy yourself
You have one life to live
And remember love
It's in you to give

As you go off
In search of new found wealth
Remember, you are nature
Experiencing itself

BREATHE

Breathe
And let your breath take you farther
Than you have ever known

It will guide you deeper and deeper
To the silence that lies within

And in that silence
You will find out
Who you are

You are divine in nature
A perfect construct
Nothing could be more complete
Than creation itself

When you come to find
The Great Spirit that lies within
You will find
Your strength

You will be noble in action
And kind in deed

You will stand up for those
Who cannot stand up for themselves

You will see this spirit
Reflected in all things

And it will teach you
To give
Without question
To help
Without reason

And to be grateful
For all that you have been given

When you follow your breath
You will never be led astray

On the path to fulfillment
Your breath will lead the way

LION HEART

Everyone faces a struggle
You know nothing about
Suffocating with anxiety
Pity, and self doubt

Walk through this world
And see it in their eyes
Betraying the light
The way their heart cries

We all have
Choices to make
Decisions to choose
Paths to take

Find your freedom
Follow your heart
It's up to you
To play your part

Let your action
Be found in duty
Surrender the fruit
And witness the beauty

Rain can pour
Falling all day
But the light within
Will never stray

The truth of your essence
Is found inside
When silence speaks
Heart opens wide

Cascade your love
Envelop the Earth
Show humanity
What life is worth

EARTH ANGEL

This body is a temple
For Spirit to dwell
A container for the infinite
Born in every cell

This Spirit moves
Through all life on Earth
Sacred beauty
Showing what we are worth

When you see yourself
In all things
There are no limits
To the compassion you'll bring

The root of our humanity
Resides in love
As expansive as the Universe
Beyond the stars above

Look into your eyes
Do you see the light shine
A fire that burns within
Candle of the divine

EARTH ANGEL

You say namaste
And bow your chin
Surrender with humility
To the light within

It will help you see
With clearer eyes
Those wings you carry
It's no surprise

Show gratitude
For such a beautiful gift
And spread them wide
There's a world to lift

TODAY IS THE DAY

Today is the day
No more looking back
Step forward with courage
Have no fear of lack

For you are abundant
A being of light
Share your love with the world
In the words that you write

The power to create
With infinite potential
Believe in yourself
Your part is essential

You are here
To uplift all things
Share your gifts with others
See the joy it brings

Never underestimate your power
To change someone's day
Teach them love
And show them the way

To a brighter future
For all beings on this Earth
To those that are here
And those yet to be birthed

We all come
From the same cosmic core
Find your power within
And let your spirit soar

Today is the day
You play your part
Create your life
With an open heart

BEING OF LIGHT

Being of light
Carved from the stars
Teach only love
For that is what you are

You were created
Divine and pure
Only love is real
Of this you are sure

Let go of all
Negativity and self doubt
Then you can explore
What life's all about

A cosmic ocean
A sea of bliss
Who knew that life
Could feel like this

Freedom to create
Expand and grow
Trust your Self
And go with the flow

You will find
Your solace inside
Diving to the depths
With spirit as your guide

You were given this light
So that you could shine
Awaken the others
And serve the divine

Have no fear
This is not the end
Share your greatest gifts
And help us ascend

CPSIA information can be obtained
at www.ICGtesting.com
Printed in the USA
LVHW012301180119
604494LV00006B/41/P